Finding My Way

A guide to help struggling business owners get back on track

Ria Lashay Ruffin Hagans

About the Author

I was born and raised in Wilson, North Carolina. I attended East Carolina University where I received my BS in Business Administration with a concentration in Management Information Systems. Upon graduating with my BS degree I went straight into graduate school where I earned my MBA in IT Management. I worked my way through school; I've worked in many different industries and have been able to assess each industry. I've worked in production to small businesses to fortune 500 companies, and co-founded Mizizi Life and Ruffin Business Solutions, LLC. I've started small businesses that failed within the first year, I've started small businesses that succeeded. My previous positions include Nursing Assistant, Medical Technician, marketing representative, call center and sales agent, distribution admin, events promoter/coordinator, IT analyst, global support specialist, Level 1,2, and 3 software support specialist, and Implementation Specialist. I've also had the pleasure to work with individuals from different countries which is always interesting.

Throughout my career I have gained great teamwork skills, a great work ethic, and great communication skills which are all necessary to help businesses succeed. Working in different industries and working with individuals of different cultures has allowed me to grow personally and professionally. I've learned so much about the ins and outs of a business from school and applied what I have learned in the work environment. After working for someone else for so long, I chose a different route and decided to take what I know and share my knowledge with small business owners.

I dedicate my success to my husband, beautiful kids, family, and my very supportive friends turned family. Thank you all for believing in me, listening to all of my ideas, helping me promote, and keeping me focused. I couldn't have done it without you all.

Finding My Way

A Guide to Help Struggling Business Owners get back on Track

      As a business owner do you ever think back to the days when business was booming and your cash flow was unbelievable? Now you're at a place where there is little cash inflow, very few customers, and you're left questioning the status of your business? How you're going to get out of the hole? How can you attract new customers? How can you increase revenue? Where do you go from here? Or maybe you're still stuck at the point of getting your business off the ground?

      Finding my way back is a guide for just that; helping struggling business owners get back on track. This guide will discuss topics such as networking, marketing, making changes within the organization, setting goals, and will even have exercises for you to do. What I want you to get out of this is: it is not the end; you've reached a hurdle that you need to get over, which you can. We've all been there whether it's in our personal life or career. But, you must first change your way of thinking. Think Positive. Think Big. I'm here to tell you there is a light at the end of the tunnel (cliché I know but I'm also a survivor of that dark, long tunnel)

Ria Lashay Ruffin Hagans, MBA

Your Vision (and Mission)

Ask yourself this question: "When I started this company 'x' years ago, how did I envision it would be at this point today?" Your vision was and still should be your motivation. The issue is when starting a company, business owners aren't setting clear visions or they let obstacles get in the way and they lose their momentum, their drive, and eventually what was once their dream is now a nightmare.

What is a vision statement? Simply put, your vision is your dream. A vision statement clearly guides the direction of your organization. Now, just to clear things up the vision statement answers "where do we want to go", the mission statement answers "how do we get there?" The vision statement sets the direction for your business planning. If you are reading this guide, more than likely you are already past the business planning, so I will not touch on that subject. However, you may not have understood the purpose and importance of the vision statement and at this point you are tempted to change your vision. Should you? You can, but remember your vision statement explains your organization's foundation so you should not be making drastic changes unless you plan on rebranding.

Let me take some time to inform the entrepreneurs who do not have a vision statement. You know what a vision statement is; now you want to know how to write a vision statement, right? Don't panic...a vision statement should not be complicated, not too simple, but stated in a way that you and your employees (all level of employees) understand where you want to go. A good vision statement inspires you and your employees to work harder, to work together to achieve present and future company goals.

- First- analyze your mission statement which is a brief description of your company's purpose for existing
- Second- while examining your mission statement, ask yourself "Where do I want my business to be five years from now?" Dream Big!!!
- Third- Write your vision statement

- Lastly- Commit to your vision. That statement you wrote (or will write down on the following page), make that vision come true. If you have to print it out and put it somewhere where you can see it every day and be reminded of it daily, do that!

Imagine a new team of construction workers building a house or business with no blue print, or an architect designing a house without visioning the end result, the outcome wouldn't be so pretty would it? Without a vision, a business risks the possibility of drifting and jumping around between tasks. The vision statement helps link your actions with strategic goals.

Examples of weak and strong vision statement:

- Weak: "Maximize our customers' ability to get their work done"
- Strong: "To build the largest and most complete amateur radio community site on the internet" (eham.net)

You see, a good vision statement provides a clear focus and direction. Let me break it down a little further

Mission statement answers these questions:
• What do we do today?
• Who do we serve?
• What are we trying to accomplish?
• What impact do we want to achieve?

Vision statements answers these questions:
• Where are we going moving forward?
• What do we want to achieve in the future?
• What kind of society do we envision for the future?

While we're here, let's go ahead and look at your company's values:
• What do we stand for?
• How will we conduct our activities/tasks to achieve our mission and vision
• How do we treat out staff, customers, and community?

What is your company's mission and vision?

Mission Statement:

Vision Statement:

Company's Values:

Notes:

Marketing

Oh, the importance of marketing and networking! The heart of your business success is marketing. Marketing is the action or business of promoting and selling products or services including market research and advertising. It is doing whatever you have to do to place your product or service in the hands of potential customers. Without marketing, your sales will decrease, you will not gain any new customers, and/or your company may be at risk for closing.

Do you have a marketing plan? A marketing plan is nothing more than creating a list of ways you plan to market your products/services. Companies who are successful in marketing start with a marketing plan. This plan does not have to be hundreds of pages long, in fact most smaller firms' marketing plan consist of a couple of pages. But nevertheless, put some thought into this marketing plan because there are just as many marketing strategies as there are creative people in this world and there are new strategies coming out daily.

Up until a couple of years ago, social media didn't exist and now this is where a lot of entrepreneurs use their marketing time and budget. Some of the most popular social media sites are Facebook, Twitter, Instagram, Pinterest, LinkedIn, and YouTube. Social media marketing allows you to further reach out to your customers, attract new customers, and build your brand. If implemented correctly, social media marketing can bring much success to your business. It can help with various goals such as increasing website traffic, brand awareness, conversing with target audience, and even hiring (well broadcasting that you're hiring). There are so many individuals out there that will show you how to be successful with social media marketing. I strongly suggest enrolling in a class (most have recorded webinars) and gaining that valuable knowledge. Knowledge is power, don't ever forget that.

Social media is great and popular but don't limit yourself. Some people prefer the old fashion way of marketing: brochures, post cards, billboards, yellow pages, magazine ads, business cards, and attending social events. More examples include email, online advertising, Google+, and webinars. This is just a few examples but the list goes on. Combine some of these marketing tactics, think of different ways you can get your name out; get creative, the marketing list is only limited by your imagination.

With effective marketing campaigns and strategies set in place, your company will greatly reap the benefits. If you don't already have a marketing team, I would suggest creating one, even if it's a team of 2, or one person who is solely responsible for marketing your goods and services. This is important as you, the business owner, can focus your attention on other daily tasks. The roles in a marketing team are designed to maximize revenue for the company. For those who will have a small team, here are a few of the roles

- Director: Leads the marketing team
- Marketing Analyst: Focus on customer demographics
- Staff Members: In charge of videos, brochures, mailings, social media and other sales /visual aids.

There's no secret to the way the economy has been over the past couple of years. It is extremely hard in this day in time for startup companies and small businesses to succeed, which is why consistently marketing your goods and services is that much more important. Do your research; research marketing strategies that are effective and cost efficient. Do some research on your competition, what are other companies doing? Are they successful? Take some time out and revisit your current marketing techniques, propose new marketing techniques, and revise your marketing plan.

Now, in the beginning of this section, I mentioned that marketing is important but didn't explain why. Think about this: your competition is only blocks away from where you are located, you both offer the same products (or similar products), how do you make sure your current customers will remain loyal, and how will you attract potential customers as opposed to your competition? Marketing; you have to persuade your audience into believing that your product is better, cheaper, (or if indeed it is much more expensive, it is of better quality) let them know that your product or your service is what's best for them. You want more customers, right? You want to increase profits, right? You want to one day expand your business, right?

Well, what are you waiting for? Get your pen, paper, phone, tablet, computer, or whatever you use and revise your marketing plan.

Advertising/Marketing Tracker

Name	Platform	Start Date	End Date	Cost

Networking

Marketing and networking go hand in hand. Networking is an activity of linking like-minded business people together to recognize or create business opportunities. This could mean anything from handing out your business card/brochures, speaking at conferences/events, contacting colleagues/other business owners, or attending social networking events. You are building relationships with potential customers or business partners; this is why networking is so important.

Everyone that you come in contact with is a potential client (or they can help you find potential clients) including family, friends, current and previous coworkers. The more people you meet and brief on your business, the bigger your network will get.

LinkedIn and Meetup.com are two social networking sites that will allow you to network with individuals who may not be in the same city/state as you but share the same interests or can become a potential customer. Facebook and Twitter are also popular sites to build a network. Facebook will allow you to create and promote a business page; you can also invite people to "like" or subscribe to your page. Using social network sites may be the fastest way to build up your network but attending and speaking at events is more personal and potential clients will get a better feel for you as a person and learn to trust you faster.

Here's an activity for you: Write a list of important contacts (people you know will be an advantage to your company) for the next couple of weeks write down every person that you come in contact with. Create a list on your pc or write their information on cards and add then to your rolodex (or do people even use these anymore?)

Now, the individuals that you are sure will somehow benefit your company, contact them first (phone, email, etc), invite them out to lunch and converse with them. Figure out if it is anything that you can do for them and let them know what they can do for you and your business. Over time just work on building your relationship with your list of contacts that you created and keep adding to the list.

The networking section of this guide wasn't intended to be long. I just wanted to inform you of the importance of networking. As an entrepreneur your goal should be to connect with as many individuals as possible, to inform them of your business, to gain new customers/clients. The best thing about networking is it's free (well most of the time).

My Contact List

Name	Phone	Email	Business

Change is Necessary

Now that we've revisited (and maybe revised) your vision statement, we've revisited and revised your marketing plan, we've created a new list of contacts to build up your network, now let's talk about organizational change. We all know that the one thing that is constant in this day in age is change. Change is necessary in order to progress and be successful. The decision to make organizational changes is a tough one and even more of a challenge to implement the change(s). What drives organizational change? Let's take a look.

The internal environment refers to the things that your company can control such as finances, company and employee performance, and company growth. These are some internal factors that drive organizational change. If your company is not performing up to stakeholder's standards, or if the company is losing more money than gaining, the company can decide to make some changes which may include restructuring, demotions, company layoffs, pay cuts, etc. On the positive side, the company may be making more money than predicted and they may see the need to expand (promote and hire more employees).

The external environments are those factors that for the most part the company has no control over. Some external factors that drive organizational change include competition, technology, social change, and the economic environment. Managers/business owners have to adapt to the changes when it comes to competition, social change, and economic environments as these factors are considered external however they have a significant influence on the company's method of operations.

Organizational change is all about adaptability and preparation. Some changes may be small and some may be intimidating. The number one rule is to communicate with your employees and colleagues, inform them of what is going on and why. Another thing for managers to do is to create short term goals and then build on them.

Keep in mind, some may be resistant to change; some also fear change. Don't; once you realize this is what needs to happen in order for you to get back on track, to increase profits, to gain more customers, you will then become more open to make these changes. Let's start on those short term goals, shall we?

Turning your vision into reality requires setting the right goals. Short term goals help you make the most effective use of your resources. The goals are often the steps necessary to achieve the long term goals. Below are a few examples of short term goals:

- Increase your marketing budget each month for the next three months
- Research your competition and brainstorm on what you offer that they don't
- Research ways to increase website traffic (hire a web consultant, redesign your website to make it appeal to a broader audience)

These are just a few examples, but once you've set your short term goals, it's time to discuss these goals with your team. Let them know why these goals matter and how it will benefit the company as a whole if the goals are achieved.

Now that you've set the goals and discussed them with the team, you have to determine how you are going to track your goals. There are project management tools such as Basecamp, Microsoft Project, One Desk, and Plan Box that are essential tools when it comes to achieving short term and long term goals. You just have to find a project management tool that you are comfortable with using and stick with it.

Notes

Implementing Changes

Prior to reading this guide you may have been resistant to making changes within your organization. At this point you know that the change is necessary in order for you to see progress. You've determined what needs to change; you've communicated these changes with your team, now it's time to implement these changes.

To make things easier for you, I suggest implementing these changes in phases. Most changes can be broken down into phases that can be reviewed along the way. Have a small group of employees try the change first to see if any errors exist and to make changes as necessary. So it's sort of like a trial period, which also gives the employees a chance to become familiar with the change and adjust to it.

Updating Technology is a common change that has to be implemented in the workplace. Keeping technology updated is critical when it comes to the growth of your business. But before you jump to the latest system/application you need to compare your business requirements with technology solutions that address them. You may find out you don't need to purchase this new equipment, you just need to upgrade your current system.

Cutting costs may be one of the most difficult changes to make, however it is necessary to reduce expenses and improve profitability. Cost cutting may include layoffs, reduce in pay, changes in health insurance plan, changing hours of service, or downsizing to a small building.

Notes

Improving Customer Service

As we all know, there is always room for improvement. I know you may think you have the best employees that provide the best customer service, and maybe you do; but just think about what your employees are currently doing right/wrong and what can be improved. Regardless of the type of contact you have with your customers, whether it is face to face or over the phone, good customer service skills goes a long way.

A customer comes in (or calls in), receives great customer service, she leaves (or hangs up) a happy and satisfied customer. That's what we want, right? A happy customer will tell all her friends (more customers=more profits). A dissatisfied customer will also tell all her friends, so let's just keep that in mind as well.

Okay, how do we plan to improve customer service? When I worked for a telecommunications company, the one technique I found helpful was individual coaching. Pull the individual to the side, now don't make anyone feel as if they've been singled out; praise them, let them know what they're doing right, tell them how much you appreciate them, and once that is done (without making the person feel bad) tell them what they need to work on and show them how it's done. I'll tell you one of the worst feelings as an employee is thinking you're doing something right and the whole time you're doing it wrong, however no one (not even management) cared enough to correct you. In this case, management needs to be coached.

As a manager, you can't expect your employees to be the best they can be if you're not being the best manager you can be. You have to lead by example. A few ways to improve your management skills are listed below:
- Get to know your employees (remember they are people first and you should treat them as such)
- Learn to correct others without insulting them
- Be more available to your employees- as their manager they need your guidance and direction
- Encourage your employees- motivate them to reach for the stars
- Offer incentives- (this I know works for sure) it gives them something to work towards

I will not stress the importance of customer service. As a manager/business owner you should already know how important good customer service is to your business. I will just remind you, in this tough economy there in no room for bad or fair customer service.

More tips to improve customer service:
- Make sure you understand customer needs
- Seek customer feedback
- Treat staff as you treat customers
- Recruit the right people
- Let your customers get to know you
- Offer specials/discounts to repeat customers
- Always know your product- consistent training is necessary
- Smile, listen, be patient, use positive language
- As a manager always be available to customers and staff

Notes

Rebranding

A change that may be necessary for some is rebranding. Rebranding is when a business decides to change an element of a brand such as a new name, new design, symbol, or logo. The only thing with rebranding is that it can be risky as some employees and customers will not accept rebranding. However, don't let that stop you. If you feel rebranding your products or business is necessary, I say go for it. Who knows, rebranding your product may yield a better brand than before.

Businesses make the decision to rebrand for a couple of reasons. Some rebrand to appeal to a new audience, some may enter into a new line of business that is completely different from the current brand identity, and some rebrand as an opportunity for growth. These are examples of proactive rebranding.

Reactive rebranding is when the company rebrands in reaction to an event that basically forced the existing brand to change. Examples of reactive rebranding are rebranding due to legal issues, rebranding to differentiate yourself from your competition, and rebranding due to negative publicity.

Let's say you've decided to take the step to rebrand your products, at this point you should know why you are rebranding. Now you need to determine the extent of rebranding (remember you are basically giving your business a makeover so this isn't something that is done overnight) Will this be partial rebranding (make minor changes) or total rebranding (erase and replace)

Rebranding takes work. You've decided that you are going to rebrand, you've determined whether it will be partial or total rebranding; now it's time to get everyone on board. It is important to communicate with your team, key players within the company, as their opinion matters. At this point you're sharing ideas and brainstorming, everyone's excited!

Let's see some results! It is important to show results early while it's still fresh in everyone's minds. Not only that, you've given yourself and team enough time to go back and make adjustments, get thoughts and opinions (which, of course will lead to more changes). Now it's time to sit back, view options, gather thoughts, and revise. You will repeat this process until it's just right for the company. Never settle during rebranding.

Alright, you've made the decision to rebrand, you've created something, recreated it, fully committed to it, and you love it, now it's time to go live. You'll have to update everything, everywhere, and hopefully it will be for the best.

Below are a few examples of businesses which have had successful rebranding:
- McDonald's: Once known to increase weight, now is more health conscious (negative publicity)
- Wal-Mart: Changed its slogan from "Always Low Prices" to "Save more, Live Better"
- Apple- Almost went bankrupt then started offering well-made, creative products

Notes

Stay Focused and Minimize Distractions

Email and internet (especially social media) has been reported to be some of the biggest distractions not only in our personal lives but at work as well. I know I've mentioned social media is a very popular way to network and advertise, which it is. However when it comes to updating statuses, posts, pictures, or more so focusing on your personal social network profile, then it becomes a distraction.

We are trying to get back on track, so now is the time for you to remove all distractions, anything that is preventing you from focusing on your business, your baby. The distractions in the workplace need to be removed or handled as soon as possible. The distractions in your personal life…..well don't bring them into your workplace.

I want you to be focused like never before. Have a seat; get your papers/pens out. Ask yourself what went wrong. How did you get yourself into this situation anyway? Identify the problem; understand the problem. Now determine the steps you need to take to resolve this problem. There is no way you can come up with an effective resolution if you don't fully understand how the problem became in the first place. Not only that, when you understand how the problem became, you'll know how to prevent it from happening again.

You may be overwhelmed at his point, but try not to panic. (I know you probably have a million "what ifs" in your head) Relax. Take a walk to clear your head….but come back!

Notes

Prioritize and Time Management

Welcome Back! Now that you've cleared your head, there should not be a single negative thought, nor "what if" question in your head. Getting back on track starts with changing your way of thinking. Know that the next few months are going to be challenging but you need to stay calm, focused, and level headed as much as possible. Say this with me "I will get back on track. I will get more customers. I will increase profits. I will not fail."

You have to stay positive, you know. Getting your priorities in order is also very important in business. As a business owner you're faced with many tasks, take many phone calls, and talk to lots of people each day and each day you need to prioritize your time and tasks. You don't want days or weeks to go by and remember "oh, I forgot to write that report," "Oh, I forgot to call this person back," "Oh, I forgot to review documents for so and so" right? No, you don't. This is why prioritizing and time management is so important. You would be amazed at how much extra time a day you will be able to gain through effective time management and prioritizing tasks.

If you have to write a to-do list every day for the next few months, do that. Learn to focus on the priorities of tasks and accomplish them in order of importance. Well, focus on what is "urgent and important" first. The last thing you want to happen is to handle all the small important tasks first because they're easier to handle and at the end of the day you still haven't looked at the "urgent and important" items. All I'm saying is plan, prioritize, and learn to use your time effectively and efficiently.

Well, well, well I hope that you have learned something from this guide. I pray that if you weren't motivated before, you are now. I know things will turn around for you I will leave you with this: Your business is your baby, you "birthed" this business, you had dreams for your business, and it's up to you to make those dreams a reality. Keep your eye on tomorrow.

Notes

Best Sellers (Products)

product	Price	Qty. Sold	Revenue	Notes

Worst Sellers (Products)

product	Price	Qty. Sold	Revenue	Notes

Monthly Goals   Month_____

Goals:

_____
_____
_____
_____
_____
_____

Actions:

_____
_____
_____
_____
_____
_____
_____

Notes:

Monthly Goals   Month_____

Goals:

_____
_____
_____
_____
_____
_____

Actions:

_____
_____
_____
_____
_____
_____
_____

Notes:

Monthly Goals

Month_____

Goals:

_____
_____
_____
_____
_____
_____

Actions:

_____
_____
_____
_____
_____
_____
_____

Notes:

Monthly Goals

Month_____

Goals:

_____
_____
_____
_____
_____
_____
_____

Actions:

_____
_____
_____
_____
_____
_____
_____

Notes:

Monthly Goals

Month_____

Goals:

_____
_____
_____
_____
_____
_____

Actions:

_____
_____
_____
_____
_____
_____

Notes:

Monthly Goals   Month_____

Goals:

_____
_____
_____
_____
_____
_____

Actions:

_____
_____
_____
_____
_____
_____
_____

Notes:

Monthly Goals

Month_____

Goals:

Actions:

Notes:

Monthly Goals   Month_____

Goals:

_____
_____
_____
_____
_____
_____
_____

Actions:

_____
_____
_____
_____
_____
_____
_____

Notes:

Monthly Goals   Month_____

Goals:

_____
_____
_____
_____
_____
_____

Actions:

_____
_____
_____
_____
_____
_____

Notes:

Monthly Goals

Month_____

Goals:

_____
_____
_____
_____
_____
_____

Actions:

_____
_____
_____
_____
_____
_____
_____
_____

Notes:

Monthly Goals   Month_____

Goals:

_____
_____
_____
_____
_____
_____

Actions:

_____
_____
_____
_____
_____
_____
_____

Notes:

Monthly Goals   Month_____

Goals:

_____
_____
_____
_____
_____
_____
_____

Actions:

_____
_____
_____
_____
_____
_____
_____

Notes:

www.ingramcontent.com/pod-product-compliance
Lightning Source LLC
Chambersburg PA
CBHW041317180526
45172CB00004B/1134